So cool!

Story written by Gill Munton
Illustrated by Tim Archbold

Speed Sounds

Consonants   *Ask children to say the sounds.*

f	l	m	n	r	s	v	z	(sh)	(th)	(ng)
ff	ll		nn	rr	ss	(ve)	zz			(nk)
	le		kn		ce		(se)			
							s			

b	c	d	g	h	j	p	qu	t	w	x	y	(ch)
bb	k	dd	gg			pp		tt	(wh)			tch
	(ck)											

Each box contains one sound but sometimes more than one grapheme.
*Focus graphemes for this story are **circled**.*

4

Vowels

Ask children to say the sounds in and out of order.

a	e / ea	i	o	u	ay	ee / y	igh	ow
at	hen	in	on	up	day	see	high	blow

oo	oo	ar	or	air	ir	ou	oy
zoo	look	car	for	fair	whirl	shout	boy

Story Green Words

Ask children to read the words first in Fred Talk and then say the word.

pool   bowl   cheese   bunk beds

Ask children to say the syllables and then read the whole word.

pas|ta   play|room   bed|room   ro|cket

bath|room   kang|a|roo   beet|root   mush|room

cock|a|too

Ask children to read the root first and then the whole word with the suffix.

pillow → pillows   swim → swimming

6

Red Words

Ask children to practise reading the words across the rows, down the columns and in and out of order clearly and quickly.

be	the	my	no
so	all	I've	she
some	want	said	he
you	your	to	her

7

So cool!

When I grow up, I will get my own flat.

I will have:

- a big playroom

- a bedroom with bunk beds – I will sleep on top and Big Fluff can sleep in the bottom bunk

- sheets and pillows with rockets on them

- no bathroom

- a big swimming pool

- lots of pets, three dogs and a kangaroo, and six cockatoos on the roof

- all the right food – bowls of pasta with cheese and lots of sweets (no beetroot, and *no* mushrooms)

My flat will be cool.

It will be so cool!

When I grow up ...

Questions to talk about

Ask children to TTYP for each question using 'Fastest finger' (FF) or 'Have a think' (HaT).

p.8   (FF)   What is the first thing she will have in her flat?

p.9   (FF)   What will her pillows have on them?

p.10 (FF)   How many cockatoos does she want?

p.12 (HaT)   What does she think the 'right foods' are? Do you agree?

Miss Hope wrote some notes about the hole in my tooth.

Mum got me a green toothbrush and some toothpaste.

15

Then we went home.

If you want a nice bright smile, don't forget:

○ clean your teeth in the morning and before bed

○ go for your check-up with the dentist

○ don't eat lots of sweets and cakes.

Sweets and cakes are bad for your teeth.

Questions to talk about

Ask children to TTYP for each question using 'Fastest finger' (FF) or 'Have a think' (HaT).

p.9 (FF)   Why did Mum phone the dentist?

p.10 (FF)   What was the dentist's name?

p.12 (HaT) Do you think it was important that Rose had a check-up? Why?

p.13 (FF)   What did the dentist do after drilling out bits of decay?

p.16 (HaT) What must you do to keep your teeth healthy?

p.16 (HaT) Why do you think sweets and cakes are bad for your teeth?

Questions to read and answer

(Children complete without your help.)

1. When did Rose go to the dentist?

2. What did Rose put over her clothes?

3. Did Rose like the taste of the pink toothpaste?

4. What did Mum buy for Rose?

5. When should you clean your teeth?